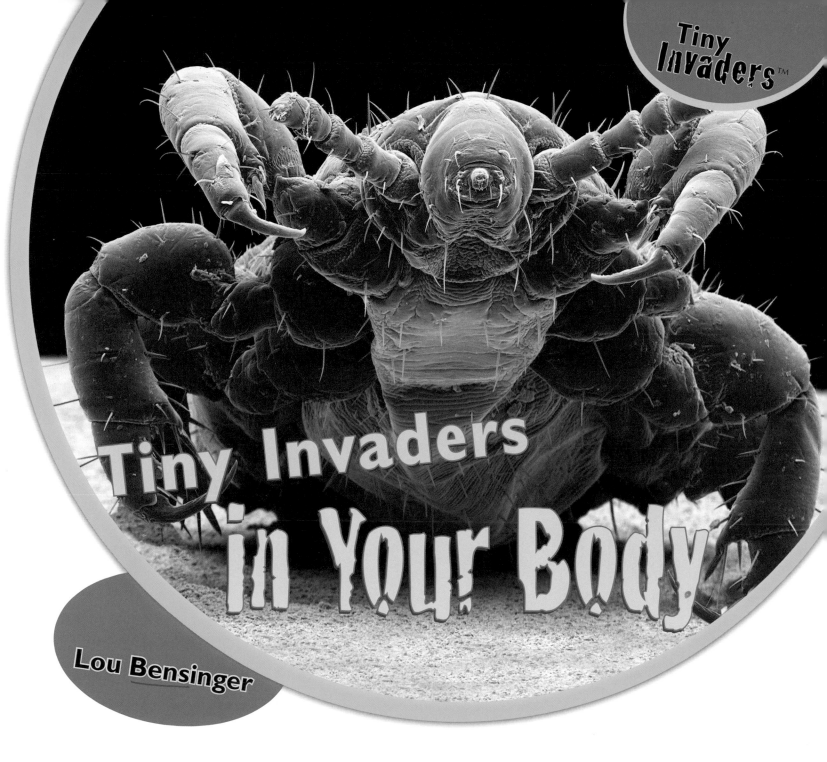

Tiny Invaders
in Your Body

Lou Bensinger

PowerKiDS press.
New York

Published in 2010 by The Rosen Publishing Group, Inc.
29 East 21st Street, New York, NY 10010

First Edition

Editors: Nicole Pristash and Maggie Murphy
Book Design: Kate Laczynski

Photo Credits: All images © David Spears & Dae Sasitorn/www.lastrefuge.co.uk.

Library of Congress Cataloging-in-Publication Data

Bensinger, Lou.
 Tiny invaders in your body / Lou Bensinger. — 1st ed.
     p. cm. — (Tiny invaders)
 Includes index.
 ISBN 978-1-4358-9379-5 (lib. bd.g) — ISBN 978-1-4358-9850-9 (pbk.) —
IBSN 978-1-4358-9851-6 (6-pack)
 1. Parasites—Juvenile literature. 2. Host-parasite relationships—Juvenile literature. I. Title.
 QL757.B475 2010
 616.9'6—dc22
                                        2009034316

Manufactured in the United States of America

CPSIA Compliance Information: Batch #WW10PK: For Further Information contact Rosen Publishing, New York, New York at 1-800-237-9932

Contents

Body Invaders!

You know that we share Earth with thousands of different kinds of animals. However, you may not know that some of those animals are living a lot closer to you than you think. These animals are not living in your backyard or basement. Some have **invaded** a place even closer than that. They have invaded your body!

Tiny **parasites** live on our skin, in our hair, and even inside our bodies. Many of them, such as **bacteria** and the eggs and **larvae** of tiny animals, are too small for us to see. Some parasites visit our bodies for a short time. For others, our bodies are their lifelong **habitats**!

Groups of many different kinds of bacteria are growing in this handprint. Scientists grew these bacteria from a hand that had touched human hair.

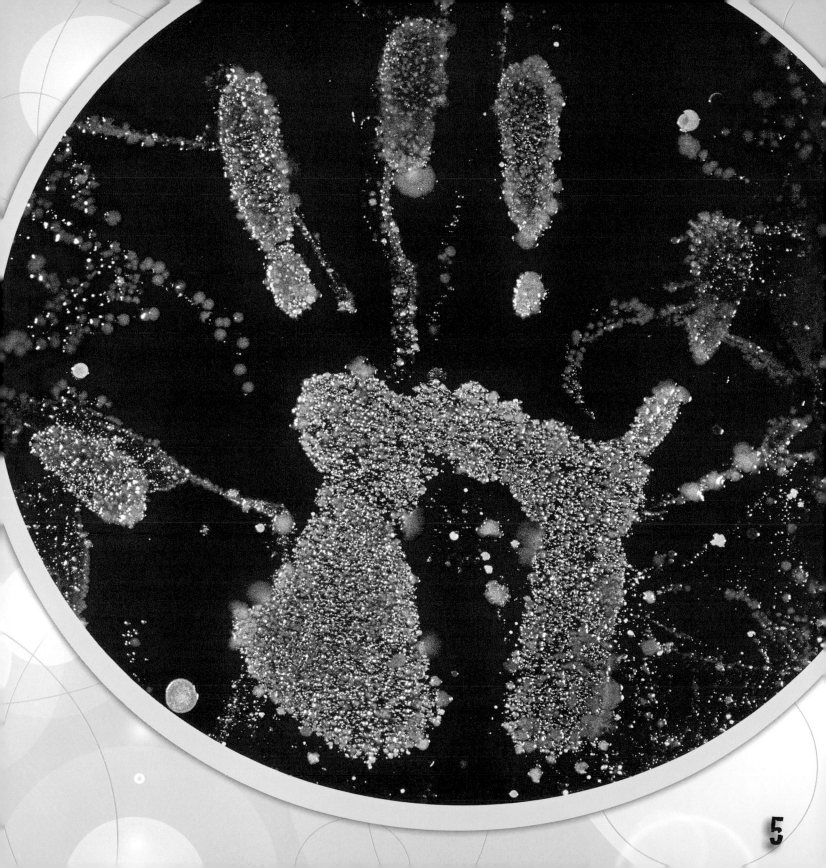

Bad Biters

There are some parasites, such as mosquitoes, fleas, and lice, that see our bodies as places to get quick bites to eat. These animals feed on the blood of **mammals**, such as people. Mosquitoes just stop on our bodies for a minute or two as they feed. Fleas and lice, however, will stay for a while if we let them!

Fleas can come into your home on your pet's skin. You can catch lice if you get near someone who has lice in his hair. They may be tiny, but fleas and lice can cause big problems. They sometimes spread illnesses with their bites.

The cat flea, shown here, is the most common type of flea found inside homes. It has long back legs and can jump about 30 inches (75 cm) high.

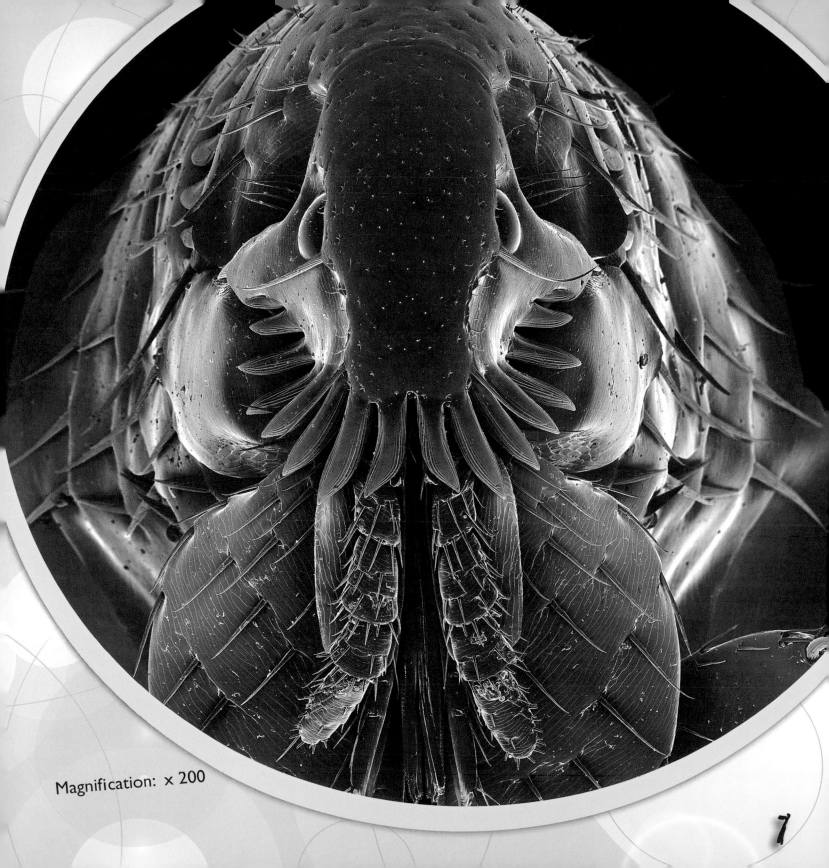

Magnification: × 200

7

Blood, Dead Skin, and Oil

A tick is another parasite that you might find on your body. There are many kinds of ticks, such as deer ticks, castor bean ticks, and dog ticks. All of them feed on mammal blood, and they can spread illnesses. Generally, ticks are a problem only during warm weather.

Mites are related to ticks, but mites are much smaller. Some live on the human body. Scabies are mites that produce red, itchy rashes on people's bodies. The **follicle** mite lives in the hair follicles of our eyebrows and eyelashes. It feeds on dead skin cells and oils produced by our skin there.

A bite from a deer tick, shown here, can cause Lyme disease. Lyme disease is an illness that can cause a skin rash and make you very sick.

Magnification: x 40

A Fungus Among Us

Have you ever heard of **fungus**? If so, then you may think of mushrooms or the fuzzy, green mold that grows on old bread. Both of these are fungi. There are thousands of kinds of fungi on Earth. Some grow in our soil. Other fungi grow on rotting trees or food. Some fungi even grow on our skin!

Athlete's foot fungus is a common fungus that people get. This type of fungus likes wet, warm places, such as locker rooms and swimming pools. When you walk in these places, the fungus can spread to your feet and start to grow.

Athlete's foot fungus sends out threads, called hyphae, that grow across the top of the skin. The hyphae, shown here, dig into the skin to get food.

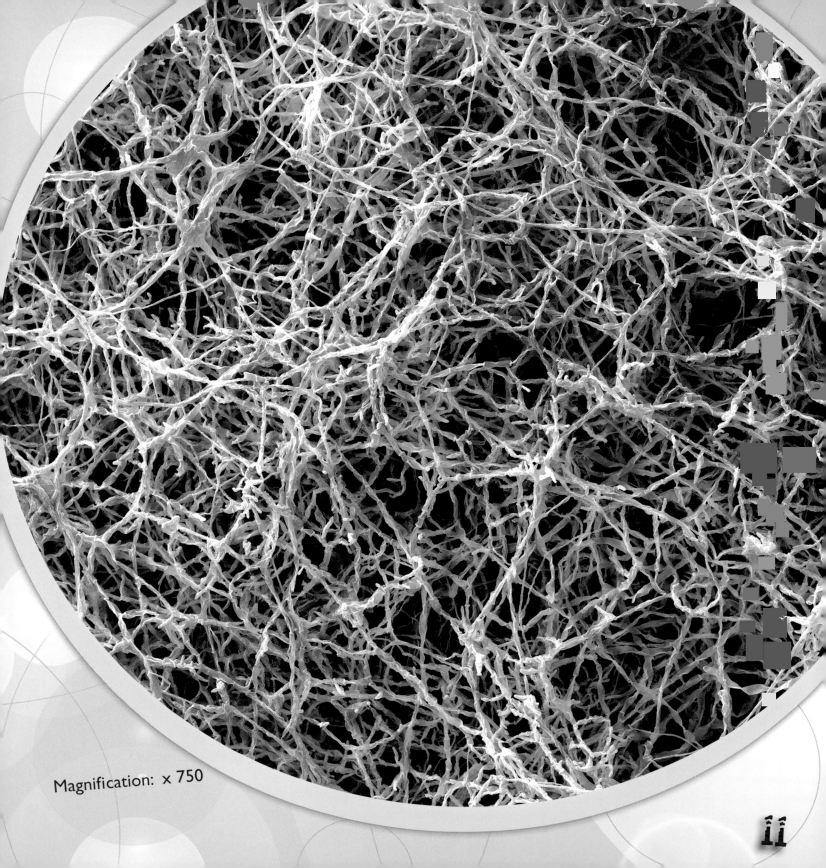

Magnification: × 750

Body Invaders: Micro Bites

1. The cat flea, shown below, has a hard body. You can drop it from several feet (m) off the floor and it will not die!

2. There are around 200 different kinds of bacteria near the top of our skin. Hundreds of more kinds are living inside our bodies.

3. The many different bacteria that live in our bodies add up to a weight of between 2 and 4 pounds (1–2 kg)!

4. An adult louse, such as the one shown on the cover, can live up to 30 days on a person's head.

Magnification:
× 70

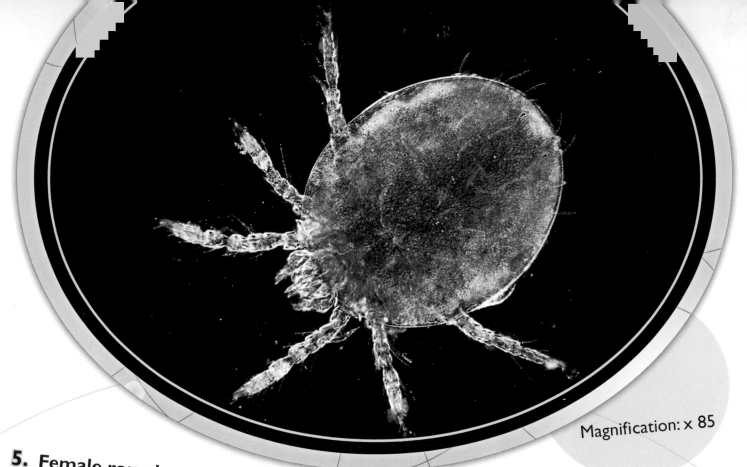

Magnification: x 85

5. Female roundworms can lay up to 200,000 eggs a day.

6. Sometimes, tapeworm larvae travel through the bloodstream to the brain and form bubbles around themselves. These bubbles, called cysts, can grow to be the size of footballs!

7. Some mosquitoes carry parasites called filarial worms. These worms can cause an illness called elephantiasis. Elephantiasis causes arms and legs to swell and look like elephants' legs.

8. A chigger, shown above, first chews a hole through a person's skin. Then it turns the cells in the skin into a liquid, like water. Then the chigger sucks the liquid out.

The Tapeworm

You may think that fungus growing on your feet is the grossest thing of all. However, some tiny parasites can live right inside your body.

One example is a tapeworm. A tapeworm is made up of up to 1,000 parts. First, the tapeworm fixes itself to the wall of your **intestine** with its scolex, or head. As the tapeworm grows new parts, the older parts leave your body with your waste. Tapeworms can often be very large. Some tapeworms grow to be more than 30 feet (9 m) long! People who have tapeworms often lose weight, have stomach pain, and feel hungry.

The scolex of a tapeworm, shown here, generally has a ring of hooks and some suckers. The tapeworm uses them to attach itself to the wall of an intestine.

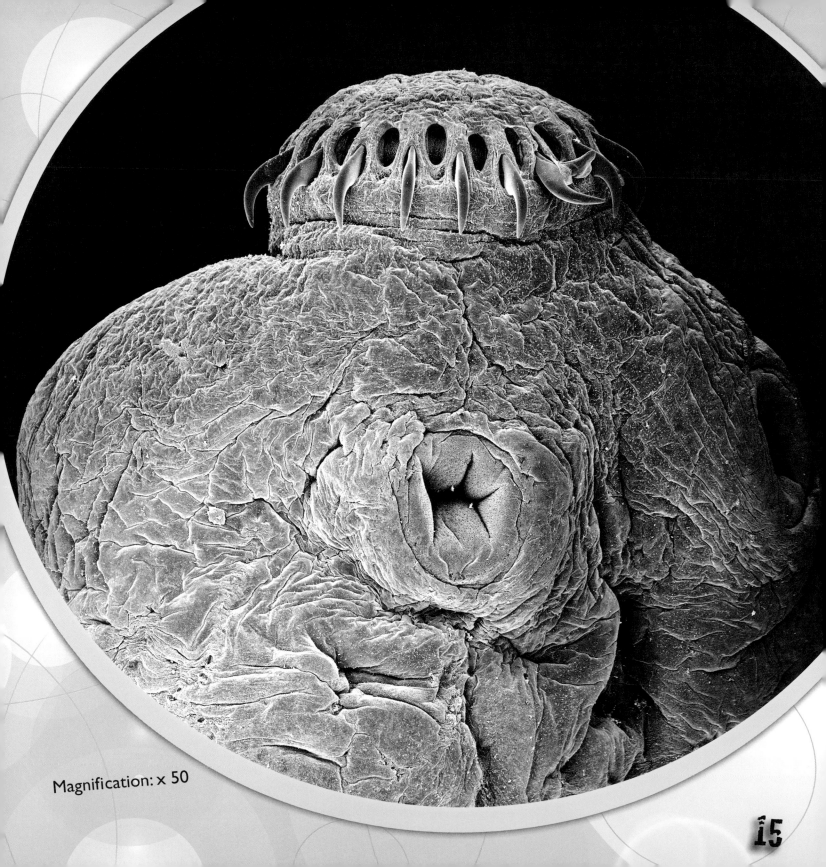

Magnification: x 50

15

Harmful Hookworms

A hookworm is another parasite that can live inside us. When hookworms enter through the skin, they travel in the blood to the lungs and throat. They are then swallowed, after which they end up in the small intestine. The hookworms fix themselves to the intestinal wall with their hooked mouthparts.

The first sign of a hookworm **infection** is a red, itchy rash where the worms entered the body. People with hookworms go to the bathroom a lot, they do not feel hungry, and they may get **anemia**. A bad hookworm infection can cause growth problems because the infected person does not get enough **nutrients**.

An adult female hookworm lays thousands of eggs a day. After the eggs hatch, the larvae often enter human bodies through our bare feet.

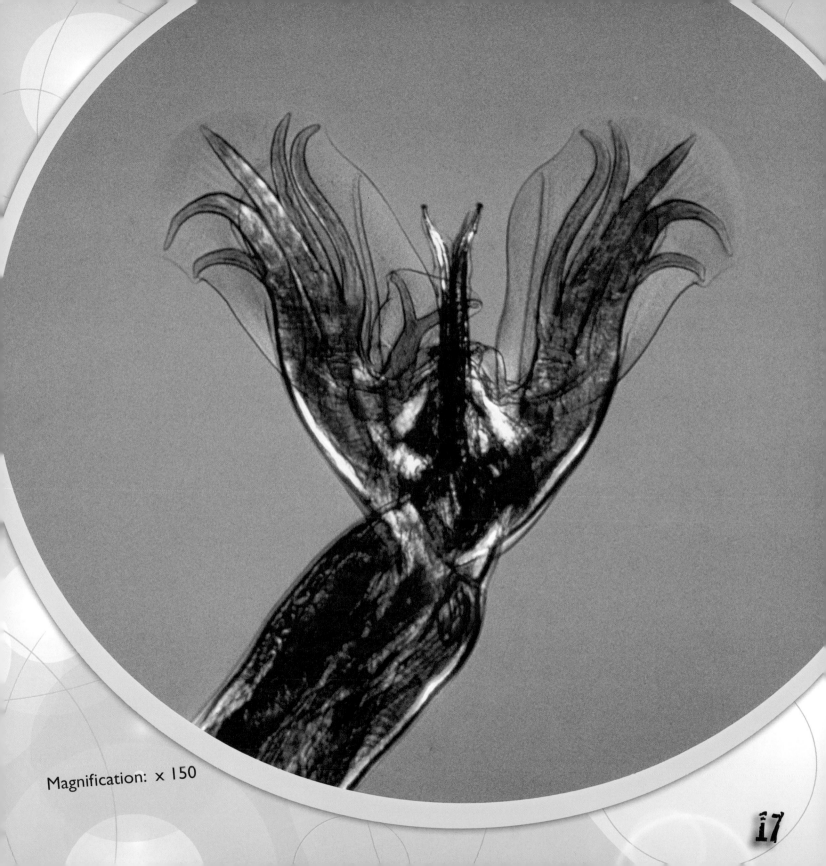

Magnification: × 150

More Worms!

Roundworms live inside the bodies of more than one and a half million people worldwide. Roundworm eggs enter the body after we touch or eat something that has the eggs on it. The eggs go to our small intestine and hatch. Then, the larvae travel to our lungs and throat. The worms are swallowed, and they go to live in our small intestine.

Pinworms live in the very lowest part of our intestine. Females crawl out of the lower intestine every night to lay eggs. The worms can then spread to other parts of the body. Some 200 million people have pinworms each year.

An adult intestinal roundworm, shown here, can grow to be 14 inches (35 cm) long.

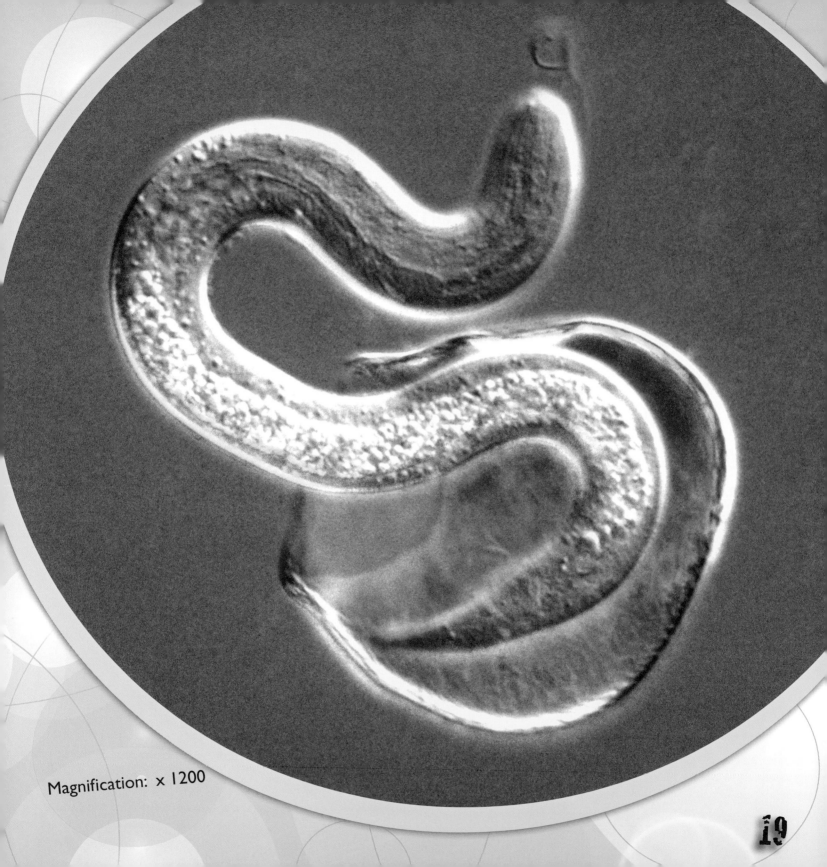

Magnification: x 1200

19

The Good Invaders

Not every **organism** on or in our bodies hurts us. In fact, there are many kinds of bacteria that we count on every day to keep us healthy. Staphylococcus, also called staph, is a bacterium that is generally helpful to us. Staph lives on our skin and keeps it healthy.

Another kind of healthful bacteria is E. coli. This bacterium helps keep bad bacteria from growing in our bodies. E. coli also helps our bodies take in vitamins. There is another kind of E. coli, though, that can make you sick. This type can infect you if you eat uncooked beef or unwashed vegetables.

A doctor can give you drugs, called antibiotics, to treat bad bacteria in your body. Here, an antibiotic breaks down the harmful kind of E. coli.

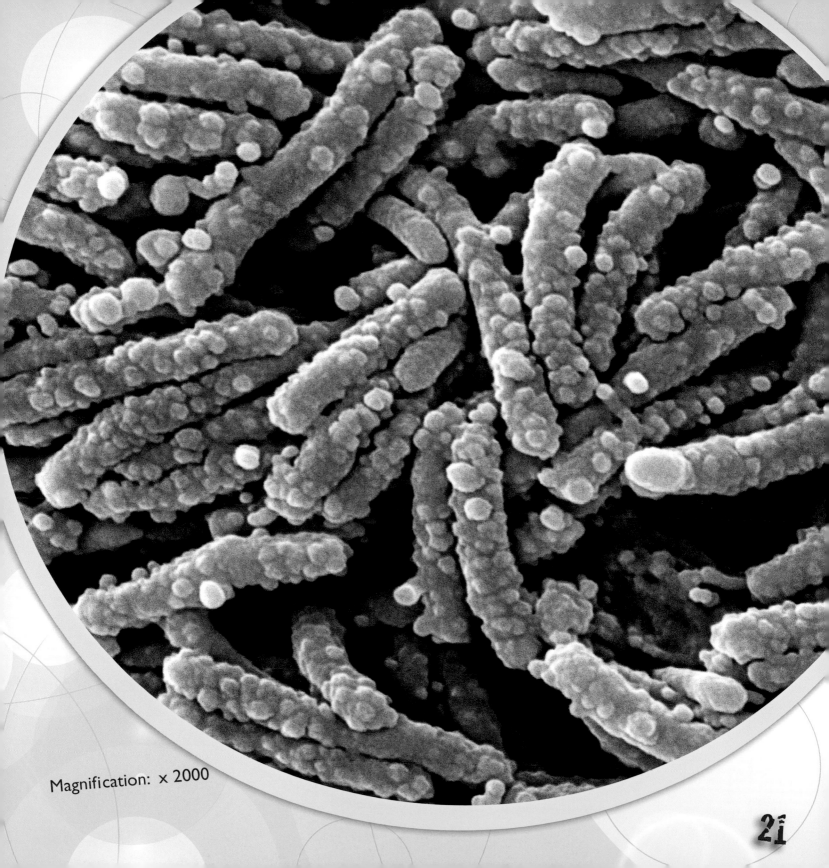

Magnification: x 2000

21

My Body, Their Habitat

Just as Earth is home to many different types of animals, our bodies are, too. Some organisms, such as mosquitoes, are parasites looking for places to eat. Others, such as E. coli and staph, are those that we count on to keep our bodies healthy. Sometimes we do not even notice these tiny animals, and many of them have been with us since we were born!

When unwanted visitors invade our bodies, we have drugs and doctors who can help us get rid of them. However, there are many other tiny visitors who do not harm us. There are even some that help us. These helpful visitors will continue to live in the amazing habitats that are our bodies!

Glossary

anemia (uh-NEE-me-uh) An illness that causes tiredness and pale skin.

bacteria (bak-TIR-ee-uh) Tiny living things that cannot be seen with the eye alone.

follicle (FO-lih-kel) A group of cells with an opening. Hair grows from a follicle.

fungus (FUN-gis) A living thing that is like a plant but that does not have leaves, flowers, or green color and that does not make its own food.

habitats (HA-beh-tats) The kinds of land where animals or plants naturally live.

infection (in-FEK-shun) A sickness caused by germs.

intestine (in-TES-tin) The part of the digestive system that is below the stomach.

invaded (in-VAYD-ed) Entered a place to take it over.

larvae (LAHR-vee) Animals in the early life period in which they have a wormlike form.

mammals (MA-mulz) Warm-blooded animals that have backbones, breathe air, and feed milk to their young.

nutrients (NOO-tree-unts) Food that a living thing needs to live and grow.

organism (OR-guh-nih-zum) A living being made of dependent parts.

parasites (PER-uh-syts) Living things that live in, on, or with other living things.

Index

A
anemia, 16

B
backyard, 4
bacteria, 4, 12, 20
basement, 4

E
Earth, 4, 10, 22
E. coli, 20, 22

F
flea(s), 6, 12
follicle(s), 8
fungus, 10, 14

H
habitats, 4, 22
hair, 4, 6, 8
hookworm(s), 16

I
infection, 16
intestine, 14, 16, 18

L
larvae, 4, 13, 18

M
mammals, 6
mite(s), 8
mosquitoes, 6, 13, 22

N
nutrients, 16

O
organism(s), 20, 22

P
parasite(s), 4, 6, 8, 13–14, 16, 22

S
skin, 4, 6, 8, 10, 12–13, 16, 20

T
tick(s), 8

Web Sites

Due to the changing nature of Internet links, PowerKids Press has developed an online list of Web sites related to the subject of this book. This site is updated regularly. Please use this link to access the list:
www.powerkidslinks.com/invade/body/